AF269850

Celebrating Earth Day

Katie Peters

GRL Consultant Diane Craig,
Certified Literacy Specialist

Lerner Publications ◆ Minneapolis

Lerner Publications
An imprint of Lerner Publishing Group, Inc.
241 First Avenue North
Minneapolis, MN 55401 USA

For reading levels and more information, look up this title at www.lernerbooks.com.

Main body text set in Memphis Pro 24/39
Typeface provided by Linotype.

Photo Acknowledgments
The images in this book are used with the permission of: © wavebreakmedia/Shutterstock
Images, p. 3; © Elizaveta Galitckaia/Shutterstock Images, pp 4–5; © PeopleImages.
com - Yuri A/Shutterstock Images, pp. 6–7, 16 (left); © Ermolaev Alexander/Shutterstock
Images, pp. 8–9; © hedgehog94/Shutterstock Images, pp. 10–11, 16 (middle); © Waridsara_
HappyChildren/Shutterstock Images, pp. 12–13, 16 (right); © wavebreakmedia/Shutterstock
Images, pp. 14–15.

Front Cover: © Volodymyr/Adobe Stock

Library of Congress Cataloging-in-Publication Data

Names: Peters, Katie, author.
Title: Celebrating Earth Day / Katie Peters.
Description: Minneapolis, MN : Lerner Publications, [2026] | Series: Let's celebrate holidays
   (pull ahead readers – nonfiction) | Includes index. | Audience: Ages 4–7 | Audience:
   Grades K–1 | Summary: "Let's celebrate Earth by picking up and keeping it clean. Full-
   color photographs and patterned text help teach readers how to take care of our home.
   Pairs with the fiction title, Milo's Earth Day"—Provided by publisher.
Identifiers: LCCN 2024038508 (print) | LCCN 2024038509 (ebook) | ISBN 9798765668719
   (library binding) | ISBN 9798765684382 (paperback) | ISBN 9798765678572 (epub)
Subjects: LCSH: Earth Day—Juvenile literature.
Classification: LCC GE195.5 .P465 2026 (print) | LCC GE195.5 (ebook) | DDC 394.262—
   dc23/eng/20240826

LC record available at https://lccn.loc.gov/2024038508
LC ebook record available at https://lccn.loc.gov/2024038509

Manufactured in the United States of America
1 – CG – 7/15/25

Table of Contents

Celebrating Earth Day

We pick up trash.

This helps the Earth.

I pick up a bottle.

I pick up a bag.

I pick up a peel.

I pick up straws.

I help clean up on
Earth Day.

Did You See It?

bottle

peel

straws

Index